What people are saying about …

COLD-CASE CHRISTIANITY FOR KIDS

"Here's a creative, clear, and compelling primer that will sharpen the reasoning skills of kids. They'll love the detective approach to the evidence for faith!"

Lee Strobel, bestselling author
of *The Case for Christ*

"J. Warner and Susie Wallace have written a book that will engage your children in an interesting new way. Helping our kids learn how to think rather than what to think is key to raising well-rounded, stable adults. *Cold-Case Christianity for Kids* will help your kids stand tall for the Truth no matter what challenges they face in life."

Melissa Joan Hart, star of *God's Not Dead 2*

"When I read *Cold-Case Christianity*, I wished it had been available when I first examined the Christian faith. *Cold-Case Christianity for Kids* combines the wisdom and excitement of detective investigations with the case for Christianity, and it's written by parents who have been training students for years. If you want your children to be ready to defend the truth about Jesus, this book is essential."

Josh McDowell, apologist and author of
Don't Check Your Brains at the Door

"J. Warner and Susie Wallace have succeeded in writing a book that is the perfect trifecta—drawing kids into the story of Jesus, encouraging them to investigate and learn about Jesus's story, and giving them the tools they need to stand by their Christian faith. This book offers our youth a solid foundation for their faith, which is a priceless commodity, and raises up a generation of Christian leaders for our communities."

Jordy and Emily Nelson, parents and wide receiver (Jordy) for the Green Bay Packers

"*Cold-Case Christianity for Kids* is a great family read-aloud, but don't be surprised if your kids want to read ahead. *Cold-Case Christianity for Kids* will inspire them to seek truth, to love Jesus, to have a new fascination with the Bible, and to become the kinds of truth detectives who can make a difference in our world."

Jeff Myers, PhD, president of Summit Ministries

COLD-CASE
CHRISTIANITY
FOR KIDS

COLD-CASE
CHRISTIANITY

FOR KIDS

INVESTIGATE JESUS WITH A REAL DETECTIVE

J. WARNER WALLACE AND SUSIE WALLACE
WITH ROB SUGGS

DAVID C COOK

transforming lives together

COLD-CASE CHRISTIANITY FOR KIDS
Published by David C Cook
4050 Lee Vance Drive
Colorado Springs, CO 80918 U.S.A.

Integrity Music Limited, a Division of David C Cook
Eastbourne, East Sussex BN23 6NT, England

The graphic circle C logo is a registered trademark of David C Cook.

All Scripture quotations are taken from the New American
Standard Bible®, copyright © 1960, 1995 by The Lockman
Foundation. Used by permission. (www.Lockman.org). The author
has added italics to Scripture quotations for emphasis.

The website addresses recommended throughout this book are offered as a
resource to you. These websites are not intended in any way to be or imply an
endorsement on the part of David C Cook, nor do we vouch for their content.

LCCN 2016946268
ISBN 978-0-7814-1457-9
eISBN 978-1-4347-1095-6

© 2016 James Warner Wallace
Published in association with the literary agency of Mark
Sweeney & Associates, Bonita Springs, FL 34135.
Illustrations by J. Warner Wallace

The Team: Catherine DeVries, Jamie Chavez,
Amy Konyndyk, Jack Campbell, Susan Murdock
Cover Design: Nick Lee

Printed in the United States of America
First Edition 2016

6 7 8 9 10 11 12 13 14 15

030918

CONTENTS

A QUICK HELLO

My name is J. Warner Wallace, and I'm a detective. I specialize in "cold cases"—*old* cases no one could solve. Many of my cases have been shown on TV. I first started thinking about becoming a detective when I was your age. My dad was a police officer, and I followed in his footsteps. When I was a boy, I entered the Police Explorer Academy. I learned a lot there, and I learned even more when I became a detective as an adult.

When I was a new officer on the job, a senior detective named Alan Jeffries took me under his wing and taught me how to be a good investigator. Alan was tough and a bit rough around the edges, but the more I got to know him, the more I realized he was a truly good man who wanted the best for me. I owe Alan a lot.

Years later, I became interested in the story of Jesus. At the time, I didn't believe it was true. But I looked at it as a cold-case mystery and applied my detective skills. Eventually I decided the evidence was overwhelming and my conclusion was this: the Bible accounts are *true*, and Jesus *is* the Son of God.

Now it's your turn to enter the Detective Cadet Academy. My old friend and mentor, Alan Jeffries, is going to train you, just like he did me. You'll learn how to be a good detective, and you'll also learn how to investigate the case for Jesus.

By the way, your family can get involved in this investigation too. In fact, you could do this together. Just tell them to check out their version of the book (*Cold-Case Christianity*) or go online to (coldcasechristianityforkids.com) to look at a leader's guide. While you're there, be sure to check out the videos and activities I've created for you.

J. Warner Wallace

You're excited to wear
your new cadet uniform, and
you can't wait to see the inside
of the police department.

Wanted: A Few Good Detectives

As the final school bell rings, you feel a rush of excitement. Today's the day you start training to become a student police cadet along with two of your friends, Daniel and Hannah. You're excited to wear your new cadet uniform, and you can't wait to see the inside of the police department.

Hannah was the first to see the school bulletin board: "Wanted: New Recruits to Become Good Detectives." After reading it, she hurried to tell you and Daniel the news. Over at the local police department, they're starting a new detective training academy for student cadets!

They're starting a new detective training academy for student cadets!

The three of you walk through the door into the police station. The desk assistant greets you. "Hello! I know exactly why you're here. I'll call Detective Jeffries for you." She picks up her phone, pushes a button, then says, "Alan, your new cadets are here."

A moment later, a towering bear of a man turns the corner and enters the room. He says, "You must be the new cadets. I'm Detective Jeffries." His voice is deep and a little like a growl. He seems serious and a bit scary. You think, *I wouldn't want to see him angry!* But then he smiles from out of nowhere and his face softens.

"Follow me," he commands as he walks you through the station to the briefing room. Detectives and officers are busy at work. Uniforms and evidence are spread out on tables. You stop for a moment to watch all the activity. Detective Jeffries clears his throat. "Ahem!" He's standing impatiently by the briefing room door. You quickly walk in and sit next to Daniel, Hannah, and some students from other schools in the area.

CSI Assignment

God also wants you to use your brain to investigate the truth. Read Matthew 22:37-38. God tells us to love Him with all our heart, our soul, and our _____.

Read 1 Thessalonians 5:19-21. God tells us to examine everything _____.

"Who wants to learn how to investigate cold cases?" asks the burly Detective Jeffries. Many hands go up. "Good." He nods. "What part of investigations are you most interested in?"

Daniel raises his hand. "Gadgets!" he says. "The high-tech stuff you see them use to solve crimes in movies. Can you show us some of that stuff?"

Jeffries looks at Daniel with a smirk on his face. "Hmm. Movies, huh? Well, we do sometimes use technology, but I'll tell you a secret about how we solve most crimes …" Everyone leans forward for the answer. Jeffries lifts his pointer finger and taps the side of his head.

Dig Deep
Visit the Online Academy

Be sure to complete the Training Activities and Note Sheets.

Start assembling your Academy Notebook!

"Your brain?" asks Daniel. One of the students from another school, Jason, frowns and looks disappointed at the answer.

"Don't frown, cadet," says Jeffries with authority. "We solve cases by learning how to think, and detectives were doing that long before the invention of gadgets and computers. The brain is more reliable. In this student cadet academy, I'll teach you how to think like a cold-case detective. When you graduate, you'll earn your Academy Certificates and you'll be able to volunteer here at the police department whenever you want."

Jason is smiling now. Obviously Jeffries has been doing this for a long time, and he sounds like he knows what he's talking about.

You can hardly wait for the next session!

Why would anyone leave a
skateboard in a tool shed?

CHAPTER ONE

Don't Be a "Know-It-All"

Start Every Investigation Like a Detective!

The next week takes forever to go by. Tuesday afternoon finally arrives. You enter the police briefing room with Daniel and Hannah. Daniel is carrying a backpack and telling Hannah about something he found. After class, he saw an old shed at the school. The door had always been locked, but today it had been open.

Daniel saw a few rusty tools and things the custodian might have used. But there was something else. A skateboard. The custodian arrived and told Daniel he could take the skateboard if he wanted, so Daniel put it in his backpack and carried it to the police station. The skateboard looked a little old, but … *still*! Why would anyone leave a skateboard in a tool shed?

"It's a mystery!" exclaims Hannah.

"Nah, probably not," says Daniel. "I bet it belongs to our friend Zoe. She's the only one around who likes skateboards."

"I bet it belongs to our friend Zoe"

Detective Jeffries is standing with his arms crossed, waiting for everyone to take their seats. He looks right at Daniel. "Hold that thought," he says. "Sounds like a cold case."

You speak up, "Yeah, but Daniel already solved it."

"Maybe," says Jeffries, with his signature smirk forming on his face. "But lesson one is—don't be a know-it-all."

You, Daniel, Hannah, and the others look at one another, wondering, *Who's a know-it-all?*

"Do you know what it means to 'jump to a conclusion'?" asks the detective.

"When you assume something before you know it's true?" you suggest.

"Exactly," replies Jeffries. "If we're going to solve mysteries, we have to look at the facts and not assume we know the answer before we gather *all* the evidence. Can you imagine what would happen if

I arrested someone without first investigating *everything*?"

"You might arrest the wrong guy!" Daniel reports.

"There you go again! Don't be a know-it-all! Who says the suspect has to be a *guy*?" notes Jeffries with a growl. His expression turns into what could pass for a smile.

"Oops!" The whole class laughs.

Then Jeffries clears his throat and says, "Or take that skateboard." You and your friends look up, surprised.

"Who owns the skateboard?" asks Jeffries.

Detective Definitions

Assume:
To suppose something is true without proof.

Presupposition:
Something you assume to be true, even before you begin investigating.

We have to be careful not to assume things before we begin investigating a case. It's important to keep an open mind!

"Zoe," Hannah says. "Daniel said so." Jeffries doesn't answer—he just looks at her. Hannah gets the hint and admits, "But I guess we don't know that for sure."

"Bingo! You're a quick learner," Jeffries rewards her. "To be a good cold-case detective, you can't start with your mind already made up. Who has another example?" inquires Jeffries.

Jason, the boy from the other school, has something to say. "Well, my next-door neighbors invited our family to their church, but I didn't really want to go. They say it's about Jesus, and they think He did miracles and even came back from the dead! Like in a fairy tale or something. I just don't believe it. So wouldn't you say my neighbors are being 'know-it-alls' by assuming all that stuff about Jesus is true?"

"So wouldn't you say my neighbors are being 'know-it-alls'?"

"That's really interesting," replies Jeffries. Jason looks pleased with himself. "But," the detective adds, "you might have it backwards."

Jason's expression changes and he looks down to the floor of the room. Jeffries walks toward him and asks, "How do you know they're *assuming* it's true? What if they've *decided* it's true *because* of the facts?" Then Jeffries points out, "Aren't you being a 'know-it-all' by assuming all that stuff about Jesus *isn't* true?"

Jason thinks for a moment and then says, "Hmm, I never thought of it that way. But how do they know this Jesus stuff is true? I mean, He could just be made up, right? Like in a fairy tale? I've heard a *lot* of people say it's just a legend somebody made up."

"But that doesn't mean those people are right, does it? We need more information before we make any judgments on the subject. Wouldn't you agree? We don't want to start with our minds made up," adds Jeffries.

"I guess not," Jason mumbles, looking down at his shiny uniform shoes.

"You asked a great question. I'm glad you brought it up," says Jeffries, trying to encourage Jason. "As a matter of fact, it's a lot like a cold case. It's a mystery we can investigate, just like the Case of Jesus—or the Case of the Mysterious Skateboard. Why do some people think the Jesus stories aren't true?"

"Like I said, Detective Jeffries," Jason responds, "He does miracles—and that's impossible."

"All right. So you think miracles are 'impossible.' Are you sure about that?" asks Jeffries.

"I never see any …" Jason says.

Jeffries walks back toward the whiteboard and explains, "When people talk about miracles, they're usually describing events that conflict with what we expect according to what's called 'natural laws.' Some people, for example, think everything in the universe can be explained 'naturally,' using only the laws of physics and chemistry. But these same people can't seem to explain the universe itself! Did you know that scientists now believe our universe began from nothing?"

Daniel looks confused. "What do you mean, 'nothing'?"

CSI Assignment

God has given us more than enough evidence to know He exists. Read Romans 1:18-20.

"For since the creation of the world His invisible attributes, His eternal power and divine nature, have been _____, being understood through what has been made, so that they are without excuse."

Now read Romans 1:21-23. So why do you think some people still refuse see the evidence?

_____

_____

Detective
Definitions

Naturalism:

The view that everything in the universe can be explained "naturally" with only space, time, matter, and the laws of physics and chemistry. According to this view, nothing "supernatural" (like God) can ever exist or cause anything.

But can we really explain the *beginning* of the universe with only space, time, matter, and natural laws? If "naturalism" *can't* explain something this important, why should we deny the existence of anything "supernatural"?

The detective continues: "I mean every 'natural' thing—all space, time, and matter—came from nothing. That means whatever caused our 'natural' universe was something other than natural."

"What do you mean 'other than natural'?" asks Hannah.

Detective Jeffries picks up the skateboard. "Can this skateboard create itself?" he asks.

"If skateboards could create themselves, we'd all own one!" says Jason. Everyone laughs.

"Wouldn't that be great?" asks Jeffries. "But we know skateboards can't create themselves, and space, time, and matter can't create themselves either. So whatever created the universe must be something other than space, time, or matter. That's what I meant when I said it must be something 'other than natural.' In other words, it must be something supernatural."

Jeffries turns to Jason. "So, let's think about this. If something, or someone, was powerful enough to create everything we see in the universe from nothing, wouldn't you consider that 'miraculous'?"

"I guess so," answers Jason.

"And if that something, or someone, could do that kind of miracle, do you think it could also do other miracles?"

Hannah gets it: "The miracles of Jesus seem easy compared to creating the universe."

"I think you're right," states Jeffries. "If the story about Jesus is true, we can't let our bias against miracles keep us from seeing the truth."

The detective picks up a marker from the whiteboard tray and starts drawing while he talks.

CSI Assignment

Investigate the most incredible miracle in the Bible. Read Genesis 1:1. In the beginning God created the _____ _____.

If God can create the heavens (the entire universe), what kind of power must He possess?

A "Tool" for Your Detective Bag!
An Open Mind

Don't allow your doubt to stand in the way of the truth, and don't start an investigation assuming you already know the answer. Be open to following the evidence wherever it might lead.

"If I drop my marker, it falls. That's the law of gravity. But who made that law? Congress?" Everyone laughs. Jeffries drops the marker but then catches it with his other hand before it hits the desk. "I'm able to stop the law of gravity from pulling this marker to the floor, and I'm only a man! Do you think the creator of the law of gravity could do even more? Could the source of the law 'override' it for a moment if he had a good reason?"

"You are talking about God, right?" Daniel offers.

"Sure," says Jeffries. "But for today, let's just agree to keep an open mind and be ready to listen and learn. Don't assume Zoe is the owner of the skateboard, and don't assume the story about Jesus is impossible. For next week, see what you can learn about that skateboard, and about Jesus. Start with the biggest miracle of all: His resurrection."

"Pretty nice, isn't it?"

Learn How to Infer

Learn How Detectives Find the Truth!

"Pretty nice, isn't it?" asks Detective Jeffries the following week as he holds up the skateboard. It's black stained wood with a white painted brand logo on the underside. The blue polyurethane wheels are large compared to the board.

You offer to help. "Ugh. It's filthy. Let me dust it off."

"Not a chance!" cautions Jeffries. "See how I'm wearing these special plastic gloves? We use them to examine evidence without changing it. I'm going to place the skateboard on the table. All of you come take a good look. I'll lift it, turn it around, and let you see all the sides. Write down everything you observe. Then we'll make reasonable *inferences*, or conclusions."

For ten minutes, the cadets examine the skateboard. Afterward, Jeffries lists their observations on the whiteboard—including some that Daniel made when he first found it. The list includes:

1. The skateboard is clearly "used."

2. The skateboard has cobwebs on it.

3. The skateboard was found hidden in a dark corner of the shed.

4. The skateboard has a partly torn old gold sticker that reads "Livingston School".

"Good!" declares Jeffries. "What's one of the first things we'll need to know in order to figure out where this came from?"

"How long it's been there," suggests Hannah.

"Exactly," responds Jeffries.

You ask, "But how do we figure that out?"

"Let's look at our list. Observations?" inquires Jeffries.

Hannah raises her hand and says, "I thought of something— Livingston? That was the *old* name of our school. They renamed it Elm Road School nine years ago."

"Now," declares Jeffries, "we have two possibilities. *One*, the skateboard is at least nine years old, because that appears to be the age of the sticker; or *two*, the skateboard is new but has an old sticker on it."

Several cadets point to the cobwebs and the way the skateboard looks. "The skateboard is old!" observes Jason.

"Good," encourages Jeffries. "The simplest explanation isn't *always* true, but it's usually the best bet. We're trying to separate what's most *reasonable* from all the stuff that's just *possible*."

CSI Assignment

Read 1 Corinthians 2:14-16. Who do you think Paul is talking about when he describes the "natural man"? What assumptions do you think "natural people" have that keep them from seeing and understanding the truth about God?

Jason looks a bit confused.

Jeffries explains, "Remember, many explanations may be *possible*, but not every explanation is *reasonable*. For example, it's *possible* that little 'tool-shed gremlins' crafted the board to make it look old, but that's not *reasonable*."

Jason laughs.

Detective
Definitions

Inference:
We make an "inference" when we come to a reasonable conclusion based on the evidence.

Trying to solve a mystery? Write down all the evidence, then make a list of all the possible ways to explain the evidence. One of these explanations will be more reasonable than all the rest.

"Now you're learning to be a good detective! You've just discovered 'abductive reasoning.'"

"What's that?" you ask.

Detective Jeffries turns to the whiteboard. "That's when you make two lists that begin with an *e*. First an *e*vidence list, and then an *e*xplanation list." He faces the cadets. "We listed the appearance of the board, the cobwebs, the sticker, and the forgotten corner of the shed. Then we thought about two ways to explain the age of the skateboard. We decided the most reasonable explanation was

that the skateboard was *old*. The evidence on the first list helped us figure out the best explanation on the second list."

"That rules out my friend Zoe," says Daniel. "She was a baby nine years ago!"

"Which is why we can't be 'know-it-alls' before we look at the facts, just like we talked about last week," reminds Jeffries. "Now—who investigated Jesus and the claim that He died and then returned to life?"

Hannah and Daniel both raise their hands. "We read that part in our Bibles," says Hannah. "We found out that there are four books in the Bible that describe what Jesus did—they're called 'Gospels.'"

"Yes," replies Jeffries, "the Gospels were written by men who knew Jesus, or were friends of those who did. They contain eyewitness testimony, and that's a very important form of *evidence*."

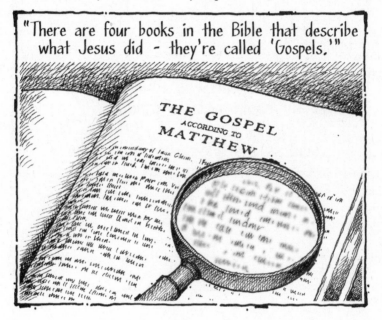

"There are four books in the Bible that describe what Jesus did - they're called 'Gospels.'"

Jason waves his hand. "But wait—how do we know these are real eyewitness testimonies instead of legends or myths or something?"

Before anyone can blink, Jeffries turns on the heel of his shoe, spins to face Jason, and says, "Great question as usual. We'll take a whole session to talk about that—but not today. We're going to start with the evidence we have and see if it holds up on its own. If it does, then we will check and see if we can trust the testimonies."

Jeffries points to Daniel. "Okay, so let's do some abductive reasoning. Daniel, come on up and make the first list of evidence you found about the resurrection of Jesus."

Daniel writes the following list on the whiteboard:

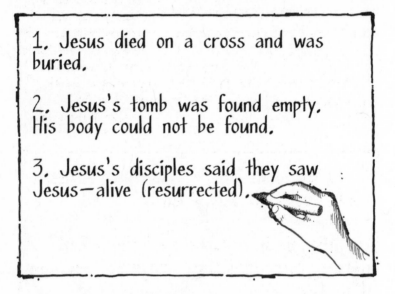

1. Jesus died on a cross and was buried.

2. Jesus's tomb was found empty. His body could not be found.

3. Jesus's disciples said they saw Jesus—alive (resurrected).

"Okay," says Jeffries, picking up the marker, "let's add one more fact we know from history."

4. Jesus's disciples were so committed to their testimony that they were willing to die for it. They never changed their story.

"Now we're ready to make our second *e* list." Jeffries hands the marker to Jason. "Can you think of some ways to explain these pieces of evidence?"

Jason, with the help of the other cadets, writes the following list of possible explanations:

"That's it, I think," says Jason as he puts down the marker.

Dig Deep
Visit the
Online Academy

The activity sheets and videos are designed to help you investigate each chapter. Take the time to assemble your notebook as neatly as possible. It's important to be organized and precise!

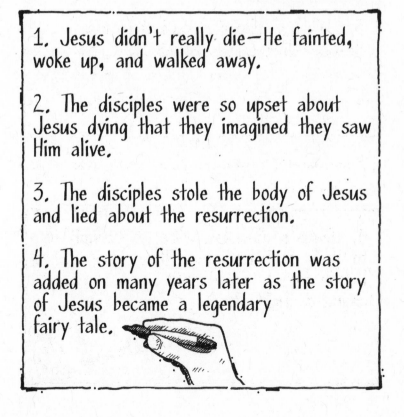

1. Jesus didn't really die—He fainted, woke up, and walked away.

2. The disciples were so upset about Jesus dying that they imagined they saw Him alive.

3. The disciples stole the body of Jesus and lied about the resurrection.

4. The story of the resurrection was added on many years later as the story of Jesus became a legendary fairy tale.

"Not so fast," says Jeffries. "Remember to keep an open mind! You forgot one other possibility." He returns to the whiteboard and writes:

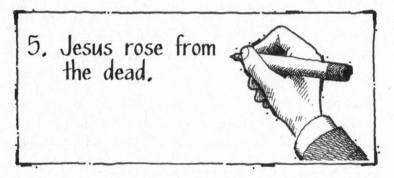

5. Jesus rose from the dead.

Then the detective shares, "We need to be fair and include every possible explanation. Maybe Jesus actually rose from the dead like the Gospels say He did." Detective Jeffries hands the marker back to Jason. He shrugs his shoulders and says, "That's fair, I guess."

The cadets begin to debate with one another

The cadets begin to debate with one another about the explanations.

"I can't believe #1," argues Daniel. "Have you heard about crosses? It was a long, terrible way to die. Wouldn't Jesus have lost a lot of blood, and weren't the Roman soldiers experts when it came to killing people on a cross? They would have known if Jesus was still alive. And when Jesus turned up later, He wasn't even injured. The 'fainting' idea doesn't work."

Everyone agrees, so Jason crosses that one off the list.

1. ~~Jesus didn't really~~ ~~fainted,~~ ~~woke up, and walked.~~

2. The disciples were so ~~it~~ Jesus dying that they imagined Him alive.

Hannah wants to mark off one more: "I don't think they imagined it either. We read that five hundred people all saw Jesus at the same time and in the same way. They could not *all* imagine the exact same thing."

Jeffries agrees. "Yes, there is no such thing as a 'group dream' or 'group hallucination.'" Everyone laughs, including Jeffries. Then he holds up his hands to calm down the cadets and adds, "When groups all report the same thing, we call that a memory."

Jason speaks up now: "But couldn't the disciples have lied about it? Or maybe somebody else lied about it years later and added the story of the resurrection to the *legend* of Jesus?"

A "Tool" for Your Detective Bag!

Reasonable Faith

Faith in Jesus is not "blind." We have good reasons to believe Christianity is true. There is more than enough evidence. Make sure you know why Christianity is true so you can explain it to others.

"Aha!" declares Jeffries. "That's where the fourth piece of evidence comes in. The disciples were willing to die for what they claimed about the resurrection. Awfully hard to understand unless they were telling the truth. Who would die for something they know is a lie?"

Jeffries looks at his watch. "Besides, explanations #3 and #4 have other problems, but we'll have to talk about that later, we're almost out of time."

Jason shares out loud, "Looks like the empty tomb is harder to explain away than I thought."

Jeffries follows Jason's thought and asks, "Explanation #5, that Jesus rose from the dead, seems to be the simplest explanation, doesn't it?"

"Maybe," says Jason. "But I'm still not sure."

CHAPTER THREE
Think Circumstantially

Examine an Important Kind of Evidence!

During the week, you find yourself thinking "big" thoughts—thoughts about God and whether He is real. You wonder if Jeffries might be able to help answer your questions, but when you meet the following Tuesday, he's more interested in the skateboard.

"As detectives," he booms out in his big voice, "we have two possible ways to find out where this skateboard came from. First, we could try to find a *witness* who was there when the skateboard was placed in the shed. Witness evidence is called 'direct evidence.'"

Detective Definitions

Direct/Indirect Evidence:
Sometimes we are lucky enough to have a witness who can help us understand what happened in the past. But what do we do when there isn't a witness available to us? We rely on "indirect" evidence.

All kinds of things can be used as evidence to make a case, so take some time to think carefully about all the other facts you might be overlooking.

"What if there wasn't a witness?" you ask.

Jeffries smiles like he's glad to hear the question. "Then we'll have to use 'indirect evidence.' We also call this 'circumstantial evidence.'"

"I think I've heard about that. It's not as good as a witness, right?" asks Hannah.

"Not true," Jeffries replies. "We didn't have a witness last week, but we were able to figure out the skateboard was old! We used *circumstantial* evidence. The skateboard's location, the sticker, the cobwebs—that was *all* circumstantial evidence."

Jeffries looks at Daniel. "I asked Daniel to do some investigating for me this week."

"Yes sir," replies Daniel, standing to his feet. "I went to Great Skates, our only local shop for skateboards. The owner, Mr. Martin, says these are large, seventy-five-millimeter wheels, used for speed.

"He's the only guy who sold skateboards with these wheels ten years ago—and they're not made anymore." Daniel sits back down.

"The owner, Mr. Martin, says these are large, 75 millimeter wheels, used for speed."

"Good work, Daniel," Jeffries says while nodding. "So now we have even more *indirect* or *circumstantial* evidence that the skateboard is old. By the way, I was in the crime lab all day, with no windows. But I knew it was raining outside. How? One of my assistants came in; I knew she had just arrived, and I saw big drops of water on her coat and hair. If she had simply told me it was raining, I would have known about the rain from the direct evidence of her

CSI Assignment

Jesus also wants us to collect the evidence. Read John 10:25. What kind of evidence did Jesus say would "testify" about Him? Read Acts 1:2-3. Jesus stayed with His disciples for forty days after the resurrection and provided them with many
_____

statement. But I didn't need her to say a thing. The indirect evidence of the water drops and her wet hair was more than enough. See the difference?" asks Jeffries, scanning the cadets for responses.

You speak up: "Can we talk a little more about the Jesus case? I was thinking about God and miracles this week. It seems to me that if God is real, then miracles *can* happen. I get that. But how are we supposed to collect evidence about God—even indirect evidence? He's invisible!"

Jeffries smiles at you and you see his top row of teeth, which aren't exactly straight. But still, he smiled! He replies, "This is a perfect example for this week's lesson. Indirect evidence can be powerful, and we *do* have indirect evidence for God. A lot of it, actually."

Everyone is paying attention now. "Where?" asks Daniel. "What kind of indirect evidence?"

Jeffries walks up to the whiteboard. "Let's make a circumstantial-evidence diagram as we list the evidence for God." He starts to draw.

You lean over and whisper to Daniel and say, "I didn't realize detectives have to be artists."

Jeffries overhears you, smiles, and jokes, "Better to be an *artist* than a *con artist*!" Everyone laughs. Jeffries continues drawing and says, "This won't be difficult to sketch out."

"First, we're in a universe that began to exist, just like we talked about before. What made it begin? Whatever it is, it would have to be something outside of space, time, and matter. We know that God fits that description."

Jeffries draws a set of falling dominoes on the board as a symbol of a universe that "starts" to exist (like a row of dominoes that start to fall when the first one is pushed).

He continues, "Next, scientists tell us that the universe is incredibly fine-tuned for the existence of life. The laws of nature and physics are amazingly delicate. Scientists have no idea why this is the case, unless of course, the universe was designed for a purpose: to be the home for human beings like you and me. It seems reasonable that God would design in this way if He created us like a loving Father." Jeffries draws a designer's compass on the board as a symbol of the fine-tuning of the universe.

Detective
Definitions

Con artist:
Someone who gains the trust (or *confidence*) of another in order to lie or take advantage of them.

Some people think the disciples of Jesus were con artists, but is this a reasonable conclusion?

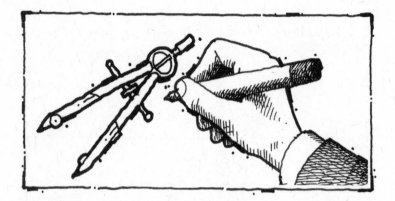

There's more. "Scientists also see signs of design in biology. Your body is incredibly designed, and you even have information in your body called 'DNA.'" Jeffries draws a DNA molecule:

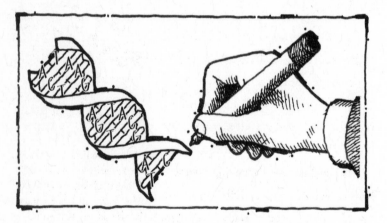

"The DNA molecule is an instruction manual for your body. It contains more information than all the books in your school library, and information is a sure sign of intelligence." Jeffries picks up the skateboard. On the bottom of the board, he finds a small stamped set of words:

"Take a look at these three words," he says, showing them to the cadets. "How do you think they got here?"

Hannah quickly raises her hand. "That's easy. Someone put them there; probably the company that made the board."

"Couldn't they have just landed here by accident?" asks Jeffries.

"It doesn't seem likely," answers Hannah.

"I agree," replies the detective. "In fact, information like this sentence always comes from intelligence. You can't get this simple sentence from

Detective Definitions

Information:
A series of symbols, objects, or letters that describe a specific idea or request.

The information in this book, for example, is written with a series of letters in a specific order. The information in DNA is written with a series of "nucleotides" that are also in a specific order. The information in this book (like all information) is the result of an intelligent source (the author). But who is the intelligent author of the information in DNA?

chance or the laws of physics. When you see information, you know it was caused by intelligence; in this case, the people who made this board."

He points to the DNA molecule on the whiteboard. "The information in this molecule is billions of times more complex than that sentence on the bottom of the skateboard. Whatever created the information in DNA would have to be a lot smarter. If there is a God, He would be the most intelligent Being ever, right? He could easily create the information and design we see in our DNA," Jeffries says as he draws a microscope as a symbol of the design we see in biology.

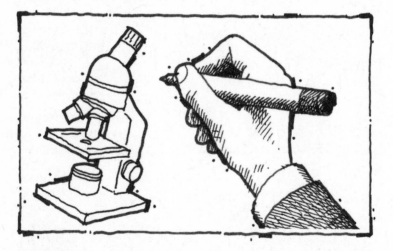

He sees the cadets and some look like they are ready to head out for the day. But he motions their attention back to him. "One more thought for today: As a police officer, I know it's never okay to steal something for the fun of it. Where does that kind of moral truth come from? Is it just a matter of opinion? Does it come from the state where we live?"

"Yes, I think so," answers Hannah.

Jeffries asks another question: "What if the state didn't have a law about stealing? Would that make it okay to steal?"

The cadets talk about it, and they agree it wouldn't be okay to steal, even if there weren't a law against it.

"All right then," continues Jeffries, "the truth about stealing seems to come from something *other* than my personal opinion or the state where I work. It's bigger than all of us. God is also bigger than all of us, so God is the better explanation for the source of truth about stealing." He draws two tablets on the whiteboard symbolizing the Ten Commandments of God.

A "Tool" for Your
Detective Bag!
Circumstantial Evidence

Remember that nearly everything can be used as evidence. There are many ways to build a case for God's existence and many kinds of evidence you can use to discover the truth about God. Look closely at the world around you to find more evidence of God's existence.

Detective Jeffries's diagram is now complete:

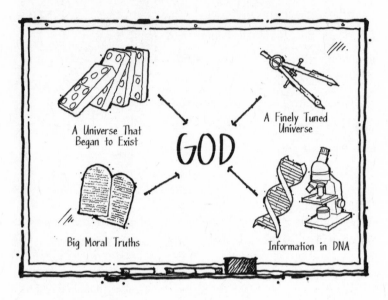

"Take a look at this circumstantial case for God. Four very different pieces of evidence all point to the same conclusion. God is the best explanation for all this evidence."

The cadets look around at one another and consider what Detective Jeffries has just said.

"I've seen it before...
at least I think I have."

CHAPTER FOUR

Test Your Witnesses

Don't Get Fooled by Your Witnesses!

"I've seen it before," says Lacey as she examines the skateboard. "At least I think I have."

Lacey is Daniel's big sister; she's ten years older than he is. Daniel remembered that she attended Livingston School many years ago, so he decided to show her the skateboard.

"Lincoln Singleton," she recalls. "He was three years older than me, and I think he had a board with big wheels like this one. He was very tall and always wore black board shorts. He moved away about five years ago."

"He was three years older than me... he was very tall and always wore black board shorts."

Excited, you and Daniel pay another visit to Mr. Martin at Great Skates.

"Lincoln?" he says, grinning from ear to ear. "I didn't know they had skateboards back when Abraham Lincoln was president!" You laugh as your mind fills with an image of Abraham Lincoln wearing board shorts in the year 1861 when men wore three-piece suits and women wore long, full skirts.

Mr. Martin stops joking around. "I'm just kidding with you guys. I think I know the boy you are talking about. He wore black shorts and his board had big wheels—except he wasn't tall. I don't remember him that way."

You and Daniel are perplexed as you update Jeffries in the briefing room on Tuesday. "Our witnesses don't seem to agree entirely," says Daniel. "Mr. Martin's description of Lincoln seems to be different than Lacey's. We're not sure what to think."

Jeffries rubs his chin for a moment, then says, "Let's talk about witness testimony today. I've been working with eyewitnesses for over twenty years, and if there's one thing I've learned, it's this: eyewitnesses *never* agree entirely. That doesn't mean they're wrong or lying. Here's a question for you: How tall was your sister nine years ago, Daniel?"

Detective Definitions

Witness Disagreement

In real jury trials, jurors are told that witnesses won't always agree:

"Do not automatically reject testimony just because of inconsistencies or conflicts ... two people may witness the same event yet see or hear it differently" (from the California Jury Instructions).

So, when you see that two gospels describe something in a slightly different way, don't panic. This is what real eyewitness testimony looks like.

"Oh, much shorter. She always says she got her growth spurt after—" Daniel stops as he realizes something. "Wow. I didn't think of that. Lincoln might have seemed tall to her back then because she was shorter."

"And to Mr. Martin," adds Jeffries, "Lincoln might not have seemed tall at all. It really comes down to the way people see things. Everyone is different, so they sometimes see the same thing differently. It's our job, as detectives, to put all the statements together to get the total truth."

Detective Jeffries turns to the whiteboard. "There are four questions we need to ask to find out if a witness can be trusted. Let's see if Lacey and Mr. Martin pass the test."

Hannah already thinks so: "Well, they both were old enough to have contact with Lincoln, so we know they were actually there. And Mr. Martin's description of Lincoln's shorts seems to match the description given by Lacey."

Jason adds to the case, "And there's no reason to think they've changed their story over time or have any reason to lie to us."

1. Were they actually there?
If not, they can't help us.

2. Can we verify what they say in some way?
We look for other pieces of evidence to see if they agree with what the witness said.

3. Have they changed their story over time?
We have to figure out if they've been honest and accurate or if they changed their story from the past.

4. Do they have some reason to lie?
Some people are driven by a bias or are trying to gain something by lying.

"Good," says Jeffries. "Now let's return to the case for Jesus. Jason, I asked you to do some research last week. What did you find?"

"Well," starts Jason, standing up from his seat, "I read the four Gospels and I see there are places where the stories don't seem to be entirely the same. But now that I understand what eyewitnesses are like, I guess that's not all that surprising."

"Exactly," responds Jeffries. "Now let's ask our four questions to see if the witnesses mentioned in the Gospels pass the test. What's the first question?"

"Were they actually there?" says Jason. "But how would we answer that question?"

"Well," says Detective Jeffries, "let's use our detective minds again." He returns to the whiteboard. "If I asked you to write a short summary of your skateboard investigation yesterday, would it include the information from Lacey or Mr. Martin?"

"No," says Daniel. "We didn't get that information until today."

"That's right," Jeffries says. "So if I got your summary yesterday, I would know when you wrote it based on what was missing, right?"

The cadets nod their heads.

"Now, let's look at some evidence in the Bible," says Jeffries as he draws a timeline on the whiteboard. "The apostle Luke wrote about the lives of the disciples after Jesus rose to heaven. Does anyone know the name of that writing?"

"I know!" says Hannah. "It's called the book of Acts."

"Correct," Jeffries congratulates Hannah. "Well, it's missing some important information. For example, Luke never describes the destruction of Jerusalem. That was an important city and he should have mentioned how it was destroyed by the Roman army. Luke also says nothing about the death of the three most important characters in his book: the apostles Paul, Peter,

Detective Definitions

Investigative Timelines
Detectives draw timelines to help them organize the events that occur prior to and following crimes.

Timelines help detectives "see" the sequence of events more clearly so they can determine when a crime occurred and who was responsible.

Our timeline of Bible events will help us understand when the Bible was written and who wrote it.

and James. He mentions how other people die, but not these three incredibly important leaders."

Detective Jeffries starts to place these events on the timeline.

"We know all of these events occurred between 61–70 AD, yet Luke doesn't describe any of them. Now think about your summary of the skateboard investigation yesterday. You wouldn't have been able to write about Lacey and Mr. Martin because those interviews hadn't happened yet. So, why do you think Luke left this information out of his book?"

"Because it hadn't happened yet?" asks Jason tentatively.

"I think that's reasonable," replies Jeffries. "So that means Luke wrote the book of Acts before 61 AD. That would explain why the deaths of Paul, Peter, and James and the destruction of Jerusalem are missing."

"Okay, but I still don't get it," you admit. "How does this help us to know if we can trust what the Bible says?"

Jeffries looks thoughtful. "Luke wrote two books. Before he wrote the book of Acts, he wrote the gospel of Luke. That means Luke's gospel was written even earlier than 61 AD." Jeffries finishes his timeline:

| Ministry of Jesus (30-33AD) | Luke Writes His Gospel (even earlier than 61AD) | Luke Writes the Book of Acts (before 61AD) | Deaths of James, Peter and Paul (61-64AD) | Destruction of Jerusalem (70AD) |

CSI Assignment

How do we know that Luke wrote both the book of Acts and the gospel of Luke? Read Acts 1:1-2 and Luke 1:1-4. One man is mentioned in both passages:

_____.

Based on these passages, which book did Luke write first?

_____.

Then he continues, "So, can you see how close the writing of the gospel of Luke is to the actual lifetime of Jesus? This gospel was written early, while people who really knew Jesus were still alive. If the Gospels contained lies, the people who knew Jesus would have spotted them. It's hard to fool people who were there and knew the truth." Jeffries folds his arms and looks out at the cadets for their responses.

"Wow, that was a lot of work just to answer the first question. But is there any evidence to prove what they said was true?" asks Daniel.

"You're talking about question #2," Jeffries replies. "Yes, we do have a lot of 'verifying' evidence. For example, we've been digging around the area described in the Bible for years and we've discovered many of the cities mentioned in the Gospels."

You ask, "Is that what we call archaeology?"

"Yes," says Jeffries. "There's more," he continues. "We've even found evidence verifying the words used in the Bible to describe people and events." The cadets look puzzled.

"Let me give you an example," says Jeffries. "Imagine if I lived one hundred years from now and wanted to write about your skateboard investigation."

"You mean in the future when we're all riding hoverboards?" Jason asks, causing some laughter among the cadets.

Jeffries keeps going. "Yes, but imagine I'm writing about you from the nation of France. If my writing is historically accurate, I'll mention you by name, right? I'll use your correct names: Jason, Daniel, Hannah, and all the rest of you, right?"

"I suppose so," says Jason. "But I don't get your point."

Dig Deep
Visit the Online Academy

Watch your penmanship as you complete your fill-in sheets. If you aren't neat and disciplined in your notebook, you won't be organized and disciplined as a detective!

"Well," continues Jeffries, "if I was making up the story from France one hundred years from now, how would I know what names to use? Think about it. In France the popular names for boys and girls would be different. Maybe Serge, Neville, or Blaise."

"Hmm, I guess so," says Jason.

"Well, the writers of the Gospels always used the correct names that were popular in the area where Jesus lived, at the time when Jesus lived, even though the popular names in other parts of the world were very different. Those ancient writers couldn't research this on the Internet. They wouldn't know the popular names during Jesus's lifetime unless they were there. This is another piece of evidence to prove the Gospels were written early and right in the area where people would know if they contained lies."

"But how do we know they weren't lying about the stuff that we can't verify with archaeology or names?" asks Jason again.

Jeffries sits down with the cadets. "Let's jump down to question #4. Did the authors have a reason to lie? What would they get for their trouble? They ended up dying for their claims and there isn't any evidence that they got rich or successful, or even popular! Many of them were put to death for teaching about Jesus, but none ever changed his story."

Jeffries sits down with the cadets. "Let's jump down to question #4..."

A "Tool" for Your Detective Bag!

Witness Accounts

Remember that witnesses can report things differently yet still tell the truth. Now you know how to test witnesses, and when you apply the four-part test to the witness accounts in the Bible, you'll find the Gospels are reliable, even though they are slightly different in places.

Jason almost seems convinced, but asks another question. "Okay then. What about the question you skipped? How do you know the story of Jesus wasn't just changed over time? Maybe the first version didn't even contain all the miracles I read about last week. What if those parts were added later by people who had something to gain?"

Everyone in the room gets suddenly silent.

"Oooh," says Jeffries, smiling at Jason. "Now you're starting to think like a detective! I'll help you answer that question the next time we meet."

You peel up the corner of the
gold sticker and discover the
initials "LB" scratched on the board.

CHAPTER FIVE

Respect the Chain of Custody

Make Sure No One Has Tampered with the Evidence!

Jason isn't the only person who's starting to think like a detective. You and Hannah decide to examine the skateboard for more evidence. You peel up the corner of the gold sticker and discover the initials "LB" scratched on the board.

"Are those Lincoln's initials?" you ask.

"No," says Hannah. "Remember? His last name was Singleton."

You, Hannah, and Daniel decide to meet with Mr. Warren, the school custodian, who has worked at the school for three years. He's friendly and helpful, and you ask him about the old shed. "It was locked up for years," he says, "after we moved our tools to the storage area in the new gym."

Hannah asks, "Did you know the skateboard was in there?"

"A boy named Lincoln gave it to Mr. Templeton, the first custodian of the school."

CSI Assignment

John considered his gospel to be an important piece of direct evidence (eyewitness testimony), just like Mr. Warren.

Read John 21:24. John said he was "testifying to these things and wrote these things, and we know that his testimony is

_____.

Mr. Warren nods. "I almost forgot that thing. I heard about it from the custodians who worked here before me. A boy named Lincoln gave it to Mr. Templeton, the first custodian of the school. When he retired, he told the temporary custodian, Mr. Jenkins, about it, and Mr. Jenkins told me. I didn't really want to throw it away, and one day a nice, polite girl asked if she could have it, so I gave it to her. Then sometime later it appeared in the shed again—and there it stayed, until you guys found it."

Daniel asks an important question: "Mr. Warren, did you know the girl? What did she look like?"

Mr. Warren scratches his chin. "I don't really remember—it was so long ago."

"Did the skateboard have the gold sticker when you first saw it?" Hannah asks.

"No, that must have been added by the girl who owned it last," he replies.

The following Tuesday, you report what you've learned about the skateboard.

"Hmm," says Detective Jeffries. "I think you're definitely on to something with the 'LB,' and you've also discovered something important that

Detective Definitions

Evidence Tampering

When someone alters a piece of evidence so it is different than it was when it was first discovered.

We trace the "chain of custody" for each piece of evidence to see if it was changed over time. We ask two important questions:
1. Who handled it?
2. How did they describe it?

We can ask these same two questions about the Gospels to see if the information in the Bible has been changed over time.

will help us answer Jason's question from last week about whether the Gospels were changed over time. Let's talk about the '*chain of custody.*'"

"What's that?" you ask.

"A record of *who* had the evidence and *when*. It's like a chain. Each person in the chain is a link who handed the skateboard to the next person in the chain." Jeffries steps up to the whiteboard again. "Let's draw what we know. First, the skateboard belonged to Lincoln, then he gave it to Mr. Templeton, who later gave it to Mr. Jenkins, who gave it to Mr. Warren, who then gave it to a girl, who eventually put it back in the shed."

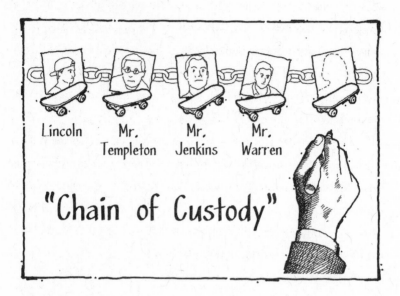

"Now we know everyone who had contact with the skateboard, *and* we even know when the sticker was added," says Jeffries.

But Jason looks confused. "So how does this help answer my question about the Gospels?" he asks.

"Well," starts Jeffries, "you were wondering if anything was added to the story of Jesus. If we could somehow trace the chain of custody for the Gospels, we could figure out who had contact with them and if anything was added."

"But why can't we just look at the original copies to see what they say?" asks Hannah.

"Great question." Jeffries pulls up a chair next to the cadets. He doesn't even really fit in the chair but leans off from it with his long legs sticking way out in front of him. "This is a tough case, because the original Gospels weren't as sturdy as the skateboard. They were written on *papyrus*, a paper-like material used in ancient times. It was good for *writing*, but not so good for *lasting*. So, we no longer have the originals. That's why the chain of custody is so important. It can help tell us what the original Gospels said about Jesus."

Jeffries stands up and returns to the whiteboard. "Let me draw a gospel chain of custody for you to show you what I mean." He begins to draw the faces of ancient writers. "Let's start with the apostle John. He wrote a book about Jesus called the gospel of John. But what if there wasn't a single copy of John's book around for us to read? How would we know what was in it?" asks Jeffries.

The cadets remain silent. No one seems to know how to answer.

"Keep in mind, we're going to draw a chain of custody," Jeffries encourages them.

You speak up. "Did John pass on his book to someone?"

"Now you're thinking," says Jeffries. "John had three students—Polycarp, Papias, and Ignatius. These men listened to everything John taught them about Jesus, and then they wrote their own letters describing the information they learned from John. These letters are not in your Bible, but they were preserved through history."

CSI Assignment

Read Mark 13:31. What does this verse say about the words of Jesus?

_____

It's important for us to make sure the words of Jesus haven't been altered over time so we can know His words have not passed away.

"John had three students—Polycarp, Papias, and Ignatius. These men listened to everything John taught them about Jesus."

Jason is starting to get it: "So if I didn't know what John said about Jesus, I could read what these three guys wrote about what John said?"

"Exactly," says Jeffries. "And that's not all. Ignatius and Polycarp then had a student named Irenaeus. He wrote about what he learned from his teachers. We can compare the writings of Ignatius, Polycarp, and Irenaeus to see if anything is being added to the story of Jesus."

"Wow," says Daniel.

"Oh, it's even better!" continues Jeffries, now pacing back and forth in front of the whiteboard. "Irenaeus had a student named Hippolytus, who wrote about everything he learned from Irenaeus. So we can look at all these letters and books to see if the story and description of Jesus is the same."

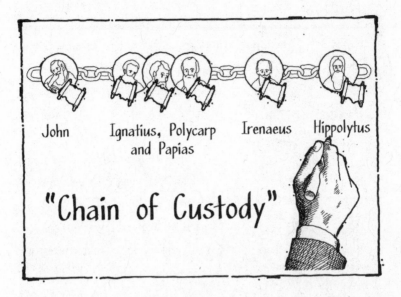

John   Ignatius, Polycarp   Irenaeus   Hippolytus
              and Papias

"Chain of Custody"

Jeffries compares the diagram for the skateboard with the diagram for the Gospels. "We know that the sticker was added to the skateboard based on its chain of custody. If we check the gospel chain of custody, we can answer Jason's question."

"So, what's the answer?" Jason asks anxiously.

"When we read everything these men in the chain of custody had to say about what they learned along the way, we can see that *nothing* was added to the story of Jesus."

"*Nothing?*" asks Jason.

"*Nothing,*" confirms Jeffries. "From the very beginning, Jesus was described the same way: He was born of a virgin, preached amazing sermons, worked incredible miracles, died on a cross, rose from the dead, and ascended into heaven. All the miraculous stuff was there from the beginning. It was not added later."

"Wow, that really makes you think, doesn't it?" Jason admits.

A "Tool" for Your

Detective Bag!
Chain of Custody

I use the chain of custody to figure out if a piece of evidence has been altered. You can also use a chain of custody to see if the message about Jesus has been changed over the years. You'll discover the witnesses' accounts have stayed the same; nothing about Jesus was changed over time.

Jeffries nods his head. "You bet, and remember when we were talking about all the possible explanations for the resurrection? One of them was that the story of the resurrection was added many years later, right?"

"Yeah, I remember that," says Daniel. "You never told us what you thought of it, though."

Jeffries leans in toward the cadets. "Well, now you know that explanation isn't reasonable, due to the chain of custody." Jeffries sits down and looks at Jason. "Keep searching. You're all going to discover the truth about the skateboard and the truth about Jesus."

Daniel's mouth falls open as he looks up to see his sister walk through the door!

CHAPTER SIX

Hang On Every Word

Spot the Truth When You Hear It!

"We've been talking about eyewitness testimony," says Jeffries. "So today, I thought perhaps we should interview an eyewitness."

Daniel's mouth falls open as he looks up to see his sister walk through the door! "This is Daniel's sister," says Jeffries. "You'll recall that Lacey told Daniel she once saw our skateboard. So she's perhaps our best witness."

"Thanks for having me," Lacey says. "I've been curious about this academy. It's all Daniel can talk about!"

"I've been curious about this academy. It's all Daniel can talk about!"

Detective Definitions

Forensic Statement Analysis (FSA)
Detectives who have been trained in FSA understand the importance of words. They read statements written by suspects, paying close attention to what the suspect says and how he or she says it. You can learn a lot by examining words carefully.

When you read the Bible, pay close attention to what the author said and how he said it. You can learn a lot by examining words carefully.

Jeffries says, "Let's get started with the interview. Would you call yourself an expert witness on skateboarding?"

Lacey hesitates for a moment. "Not really. I mean, I never actually owned a skateboard. My mom didn't think they were safe."

"Now, Lacey," asks Jeffries, "why did you specifically remember *this* skateboard?"

"The large poly wheels make the board ride really fast." Lacey points to the blue wheels. "It's a smooth riding board too."

"How often did you see your friend Lincoln skating on this board?"

Lacey responds, "I was—um, I mean, Lincoln was on it almost every day."

Jeffries ends the interview here. "Thank you, Lacey. Feel free to have a seat and join our discussion. Cadets, I hope you were listening closely, because today we're going to talk about 'hanging on every word'—listening to what is said, how it is said, and also what is *not* said. Much of the time, we don't listen well, you know," adds Jeffries.

"You sound like my teacher." Hannah sighs, and everybody laughs.

Jeffries keeps the conversation going. "Your teacher sounds like a good detective, Hannah. Listening is key! We're trying to collect evidence—as much as we can, from wherever we can find it. When someone answers a question, listen for *what* they say. But also listen for *how* they say it. The words they use, or decide *not* to use, and the way they describe things. Remember, every speaker or writer has a choice when it comes to words. Their choices can tell us a lot about what happened. Words can even be *evidence!*"

Jeffries smiles slyly. "In fact, I think you all may have received another clue or two about that mysterious skateboard, if you were listening carefully."

You and Daniel exchange glances. He raises his eyebrows; you shrug. What clue is Jeffries talking about? Daniel does think it's odd that Lacey knew so much about skateboards when she never actually owned one, but he's not sure what he might have missed.

"We're also looking into the case for Jesus," continues Jeffries. "And we have a great opportunity to listen very closely to the eyewitnesses. These witnesses have been dead a long time, but we do have their testimonies, and we have them in great detail.

"Let's take a look, for example, at the gospel of Mark. Papias, that student of John I was telling you about, once said Mark wrote the gospel based on the preaching of Peter. In other words, Mark's gospel is actually Peter's eyewitness statement."

"Mark was Peter's 'scribe'—he wrote down Peter's teaching, so he's the actual author."

"Why isn't it just called the gospel of Peter then?" asks Jason.

"Because Mark was Peter's 'scribe'—he wrote down Peter's teaching, so *he's* the actual author." Jeffries can tell that Jason isn't satisfied with that answer.

"How can you be so sure Mark's gospel contains Peter's information?" asks Jason.

"Well," says Jeffries, "one way is to look at how Mark writes his gospel and the words he uses. Remember, words can be *evidence*!"

Jeffries picks up his marker. "Let's talk about some *word* evidence and make another circumstantial evidence diagram." Jeffries takes a Bible from his desk, flips a few pages, then looks up and says, "If you'll listen carefully to what Mark says the next time you read his book, you'll find several interesting things:

1. Peter is a major character in Mark's gospel.

2. Mark writes about Peter as a friend.

3. Mark treats Peter kindly.

4. Mark shares little things only Peter would know.

5. Mark seems to know a lot about Peter's preaching.

"1. Peter is a major character in Mark's gospel.
For example, Mark's gospel mentions Peter *a lot*
more than Matthew's gospel. That makes sense if
Peter is the one telling Mark about Jesus. If that's
true, we would *expect* to read more about Peter in
Mark's gospel." Detective Jeffries draws a calculator
on the whiteboard as a symbol of how often Mark
mentions Peter:

"2. Mark writes about Peter as a friend. The
other gospels refer to Peter by his full name—
'Simon Peter'—but Mark just calls him 'Peter.'
That makes sense, too, if Mark is Peter's special
scribe." Jeffries now draws the word "PETER" on
the whiteboard:

"**3. Mark treats Peter kindly.** Mark seldom says anything unkind about Peter, even when Peter makes a silly mistake. That may also be good evidence that Mark is writing down the words of someone he sees as a friend." Detective Jeffries next draws a heart on the whiteboard to represent how kindly Mark treats Peter:

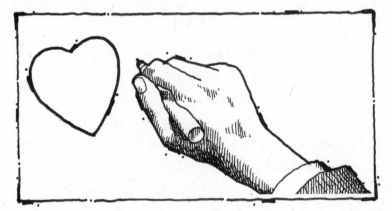

"4. Mark shares little things only Peter would know. In many places in Mark's gospel, there are small, almost unimportant details that only Peter would have known. This makes sense if Mark was listening carefully to Peter's story." Jeffries draws an image of a magnifying glass as a symbol of the detail that Mark includes:

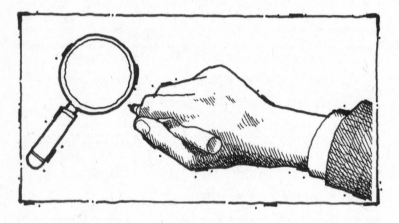

"5. Mark seems to know a lot about Peter's preaching. Mark's gospel is different than some of the other gospels—he doesn't, for example, include the story of how Jesus was born. Mark's brief style is very similar to a sermon Peter later gave in the book of Acts. This may also be evidence of Mark's friendship with Peter." Lastly, Detective Jeffries draws a picture of a microphone to symbolize the way Mark seems to know Peter's preaching:

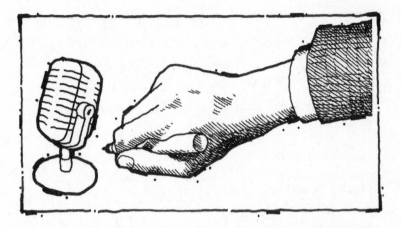

Detective Jeffries draws the five different kinds of word evidence on the whiteboard:

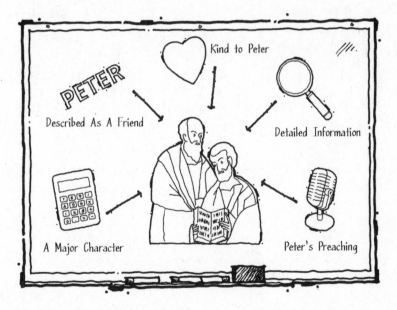

A "Tool" for Your

Detective Bag!

Words Matter

Remember the importance of words every time you read the Bible. Why did the writer use the particular word he used? Was there some other word he could have used? Why did he use *that* word? Look at words as *evidence.* Take your time and think about words from now on.

He says, "Are you starting to see how we can use this kind of evidence to make a case? When we start paying attention to Mark's choice of words, we discover things we might have missed if we weren't paying close attention."

Detective Jeffries turns to Jason. "There are very good reasons to believe that Simon Peter, the fisherman who followed Jesus, shared his memories with a writer named Mark. And that means Mark's gospel is important to us as we are trying to understand the truth about Jesus."

Jason looks impressed. He wonders, though, if he might have missed something when Lacey gave her statement about the skateboard.

The more he examines the board,
the more he finds.

CHAPTER SEVEN

Separate Artifacts from Evidence

Clean Up Your Crime Scene!

The Student Cadet Academy is approaching its final two weeks, so Jason takes the skateboard home as he carefully considers what Lacey told the class. The more he examines the board, the more he finds. On the top edge of the board he sees a thin swirl of white paint and several tiny white paint drops. He returns to the briefing room the following week, hoping his discovery might help solve the mystery.

"Has anyone else noticed this paint mark and these droplets?" Jason asks.

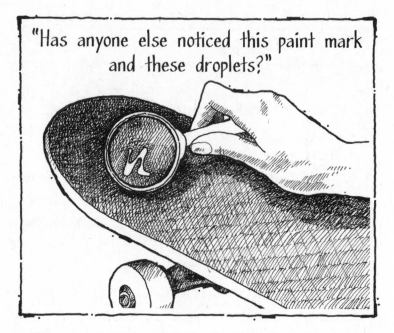

"Has anyone else noticed this paint mark and these droplets?"

"You mean this 'squiggly'?" asks Hannah, pointing to the swirling mark.

"Squiggly?" questions Daniel.

"I missed the class on squiggly evidence," you say.

Hannah points to the swirling paint mark and says, "I never noticed it before, but there it is: a white squiggly!"

Everyone wants a look, and sure enough, everyone now notices the swirling paint mark. "What would *you* call that?" Hannah asks.

"'Squiggly' works for me." Jeffries shrugs, and everybody laughs.

Jason wants to investigate further. "Can we have Lacey come back so we can ask her about this paint?"

"I don't think we need to," says Daniel. "When I first saw the skateboard, it was sitting next to an old can of white paint, and I saw similar 'squigglies' and paint drops on the tools next to the board."

"Sounds like the paint is something *other* than evidence," says Jeffries.

"What do you mean?" asks Jason.

Jeffries lowers his voice and takes a serious tone: "Every time I enter a crime scene … I expect to find two kinds of objects."

The cadets lean forward to hear what Jeffries has to say. You've been waiting for Jeffries to share something about a real crime scene.

Jeffries continues, "Evidence and *artifacts*."

Detective Definitions

Artifacts and Evidence

Detectives are never alarmed to find artifacts in the crime scene alongside evidence. In fact, they expect to find things that are important to the case, and stuff that isn't. It's the detective's job to learn the difference and separate one from the other.

"I was hoping for something a bit more dramatic," says Jason.

Jeffries picks up the skateboard and examines it carefully. "Sorry to disappoint you, Jason, but the paint on the skateboard appears to be an *artifact* rather than a piece of *evidence.*"

"What's an 'artifact'?" you ask.

Jeffries explains, "Evidence is all the stuff that's *related to* the crime or mystery we're investigating. Artifacts are the things that *aren't related to* the case at all." Jeffries points to the paint on the skateboard. "This paint was most likely spilled on the board after it was finally left in the shed. It's not evidence and it can't tell us anything about the owner. It's an *artifact.*"

Jason looks disappointed.

Jeffries pulls his chair alongside Jason. "Don't be discouraged. It's superimportant to separate the artifacts from the evidence, so your discovery is valuable." Jeffries pulls out his Bible. "I have to separate artifacts from evidence in every crime scene I work, and scholars also do this in the Bible."

"What do you mean?" asks Daniel.

Jeffries opens one of the Gospels and says, "Remember, we don't have any of the original copies of these books. Instead we have copies that were made before the originals wore out. The first believers made many copies and sometimes these old copies don't match."

"If that's true," says Jason, "we can't really trust the Bible. It might contain all kinds of errors!" All the cadets sit silently. Jason looks around the room. "How can we trust what the Bible says about Jesus if there are differences in the old copies?"

"That's another one of your great questions, Jason," answers Jeffries. "We need to

CSI Assignment

God wants us to investigate the Bible so we will trust it and rely on it.

Read Matthew 4:4. To what does God compare His words?

think like detectives and separate the artifacts from evidence." He stands and walks over to the whiteboard.

"I don't get it," you say.

"Let me explain," responds Jeffries. "Scribes made the copies of the original Gospels and sometimes they mistakenly changed a letter or a word. Some scribes even *added* a word or set of words. They weren't necessarily trying to change the message. Usually they were just trying to make something easier to understand."

Scribes made the copies of the original gospels

Jeffries starts to write on the whiteboard. "In the gospel of John, for example, one ancient copy says something slightly different than another ancient copy":

"That doesn't seem like a big deal," you say.

"You're right," Jeffries responds. "None of the changes affect anything we know about Jesus."

Jason is not so sure. "But how come your Bible only uses one of these two sentences? How did the 'scholars' decide which one was correct?"

"They were thinking like detectives!" exclaims Jeffries loudly, causing the cadets to jump in their seats. "They simply compared copies, and the more copies you have to compare, the more likely you are to find the truth."

"I *still* don't get it," says Jason. He looks like he *wants* to understand but still seems to be struggling.

"Okay," states Jeffries. "Let me illustrate it for you." He writes the following sentence on the whiteboard:

If Ja on is a go8d defective, he will sta !

"Imagine we found an ancient papyrus with this mixed-up message. What does it say?"

"I'm not sure," admits Jason.

"I don't blame you," says Jeffries. "Whoever copied the original left out some letters and even put in a number that doesn't belong. But what if I found two other ancient altered copies of this sentence and compared them to the first?" Detective Jeffries now writes two more sentences below the first:

If Ja on is a go8d defective, he will sta !

If Jaso os a good detecti e, he ill s and!

If ason s a good betective, he wil   tand!

"Can you figure out what the original sentence must have said by comparing these three messed-up copies?" asks Jeffries.

Jason reads the three sentences carefully, one directly above the other. He slowly pushes back his chair and stands up. Everyone claps and cheers for him.

Dig Deep
Visit the Online Academy

You're getting close to completing your Academy Notebook. Be sure to stay up with the additional activities and get ready to graduate after the next chapter!

Jason reads the three sentences carefully...
He slowly pushes back his chair and stands up

"Good job, Jason!" says Jeffries. "You were able to figure out what the original said, even though you had two inaccurate copies. You compared the copies and were able to separate the *artifacts*—the stuff that *wasn't* part of the original statement—from the *evidence*—the stuff that *was* part of the original statement."

Jason proudly smiles and sits back down.

"Now," continues Jeffries, "imagine that you had hundreds of copies of this sentence, instead of just two. Do you think you'd be able to figure out what the original said?"

"Sure," says Jason.

"Well, scholars and Bible experts have thousands of ancient copies of the Bible documents to compare to one another—more ancient copies than any other book in history. It's an amazing collection of early documents. They've compared them the same way you compared those three sentences. You figured out what the original message said even though the copies you had were slightly altered. You were sure enough about the original message to stand up, right?"

"Yes sir," says Jason.

Jeffries smiles. "Then we can figure out the original message of the Gospels using the same detective technique. That's why you can be sure enough about the words in this Bible to take a stand for Jesus."

A "Tool" for Your

Detective Bag!

Expect Artifacts

Don't be surprised to find artifacts in our Bible. Most Bibles identify variations in the ancient copies by putting a note at the side or bottom of the page. Be a good detective and focus on the evidence instead of the artifacts. You can trust what your Bible says about Jesus.

"I still have my doubts about the case for Jesus..."

CHAPTER EIGHT

Resist Conspiracy Theories

Discover Why Lies Are Hard to Keep!

The final day of the academy has arrived. Jason spent the entire week thinking about what Jeffries said.

"I still have my doubts about the case for Jesus," he tells the cadets before Jeffries enters the briefing room. "What if the disciples who wrote about Jesus were all just lying? Even if the Gospels were written early and haven't changed over time, and even if we can sort out any little additions or changes that might have been made, I still wonder if the whole thing isn't just a big lie."

"...I still wonder if the whole thing isn't just a big lie."

Detective Definitions

Conspiracy

When two or more people work together to do something harmful or illegal and then lie about it so no one will find out.

There's a difference between a conspiracy and a successful conspiracy. If you think you know about a successful conspiracy, it wasn't successful! If it had been, you wouldn't know about it!

Successful conspiracies are incredibly hard to pull off because they require the four things described by Detective Jeffries in this chapter.

You think of something important and say, "But remember what Jeffries said about the fact that the disciples didn't have a good *reason* to lie? Why would they all choose to suffer like they did if they were only lying?"

Jeffries enters the room before Jason can answer. He's holding a stack of graduation certificates. "Well, it's almost time to graduate from the academy, but I want to cover one more important issue with you." He points to the skateboard. "How can we be sure that there really is a mystery to solve here?"

Daniel is surprised by Jeffries's question. "What do you mean? We still don't know who owned the skateboard, right?"

Jeffries raises a finger. "But what if the entire story about the skateboard is a lie? What if all the information you got from Mr. Warren, Mr. Martin, and Lacey is untrue?"

"You mean like a conspiracy?" asks Hannah.

"That's right," continues Jeffries. "What if they made it all up and they simply put that skateboard in the shed to create a story?"

"That doesn't make any sense," says Jason. "That would mean all of them were lying. That seems crazy."

"I think you're right about that," says Jeffries as he returns to the whiteboard.

1. A small number of conspirators.

2. Great communication.

3. A short time span.

4. Close friendships.

5. Low pressure.

"Conspiracies occur when groups of people commit a crime, or tell a lie, and then try to keep the secret *forever*. I've investigated many conspiracy cases, so I know you need five things to pull one off successfully:"

1. A small number of conspirators. It's a lot easier for two people to tell the same lie and keep a secret than it is for twenty people to do the same. The more people who are involved, the more likely someone will make a mistake.

2. Great communication. It's harder than it sounds for conspirators to keep their stories straight. If they are questioned separately, they need to be able to find out what the other conspirators said.

3. A short time span. It's harder to tell a lie for a year than it is to tell it for a day.

4. Close friendships. The closer the relationship between conspirators, the better. People don't usually "tell on" their best friends.

5. Low pressure. If no one puts any pressure on the people telling the lie, they might get away with it. The less pressure, the easier it is to keep a secret.

"Now let's apply these five concepts to the case for Jesus," declares Jeffries.

You are glad Jeffries is talking about this: "Jason was just wondering if the disciples all lied about Jesus," you say.

Jeffries nods. "Well, let's look at that. How large was the group of conspirators?"

"Just twelve," says Jason.

"You didn't think three people could pull off the conspiracy about the skateboard, but you think twelve could pull off a conspiracy about Jesus? Were the twelve disciples the only ones who saw Jesus resurrected? Remember what Hannah said a few weeks ago? There were five hundred people who said they saw Jesus all at one time."

"That's right," says Hannah. "That does seem like *way* too many."

"And how could all these people stay in touch with each other to get their stories lined up, especially since they were scattered all over the Roman Empire?"

"I guess they couldn't text or call each other on the phone," says Daniel. Everyone laughs.

"And they held their story together for over fifty years!" says Jeffries as he continues down the whiteboard list. "Worse yet, they suffered

CSI Assignment

How many people would have been involved in a conspiracy to lie about the resurrection?

Read Acts 1:12-26. How many people (who knew Jesus from the baptism to the resurrection) were in the upper room?

Read 1 Corinthians 15:3-7. How many people saw Jesus risen from the dead?

Is it reasonable to believe this many people could keep a secret?

like we described a few weeks ago. They were under incredible pressure to change their story, but they never did. Are you all starting to see the problems with this 'conspiracy theory'?"

"Yes, but they were good friends, right?" asks Jason. "Maybe that helped them stick to their lie."

"Well, that doesn't explain Matthew, does it?" replies Jeffries. "He wasn't raised around the other disciples and wasn't their friend when he met Jesus. Instead, he was a tax collector named Levi, disliked by the others. Why would he lie to protect them when times got tough?"

"Hmm," says Jason.

 Jeffries walks toward the briefing room door and says, "Think about that for a minute while we wrap up the mystery of the skateboard." He opens the door, and in walks Lacey! "As it turns out, Lacey is the key to solving our mystery."

Suddenly it dawns on you. Daniel's last name is Bolan. That means Lacey's last name is *also* Bolan. The letters under the sticker on the board were *LB*.

"*You* owned the skateboard!" you yell out.

"Good work," says Lacey.

"Why didn't you tell us?" Daniel asks.

"Because Detective Jeffries told me not to," she explains. "Once he solved it, he asked me to play along and let you guys try to figure it out on your own. I kept the board in the shed since I couldn't bring it home, and carved my initials so it wouldn't be stolen. Then I put that sticker over the initials because I was graduating and didn't want our parents to somehow see the board with my initials on it."

"I wondered how you knew so much about skateboards," Daniel says.

"Lincoln was older than me," Lacey admits, "and I always wanted his skateboard, so I asked Mr. Warren if I could have it. I loved riding it because it was fast and smooth. I knew Mom

A "Tool" for Your Detective Bag!

Group Lies

Movies and books that describe incredible conspiracies are popular, but now you know why they are unreasonable. Don't get caught up in crazy theories, especially when people claim the disciples lied about Jesus.

wouldn't approve, and that made me feel guilty. I ended up telling our parents later on."

Jeffries is delighted that the cadets finally see how the pieces of the puzzle fit together. "Just like there was enough evidence in this mystery to figure out who owned the skateboard, there's also enough evidence to figure out the truth about Jesus."

Jeffries starts one last list on the whiteboard. "The Gospels passed the test for reliable eyewitnesses":

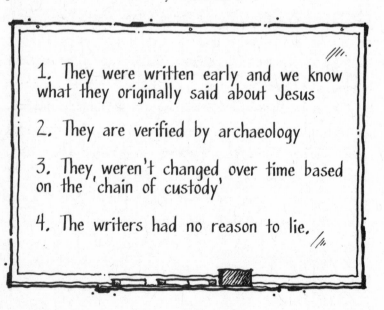

1. They were written early and we know what they originally said about Jesus

2. They are verified by archaeology

3. They weren't changed over time based on the 'chain of custody'

4. The writers had no reason to lie.

Jeffries continues, "We also have good reason to believe the Bible is telling us the truth about the resurrection":

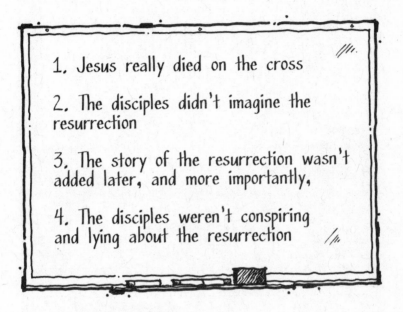

1. Jesus really died on the cross

2. The disciples didn't imagine the resurrection

3. The story of the resurrection wasn't added later, and more importantly,

4. The disciples weren't conspiring and lying about the resurrection

"Wow, I guess we really did learn a lot about evidence!" exclaims Hannah.

"Yes. In fact, I think you've all learned enough to graduate from the Student Cadet Academy!" announces Jeffries. Then he calls each cadet to the front of the room to receive their certificates.

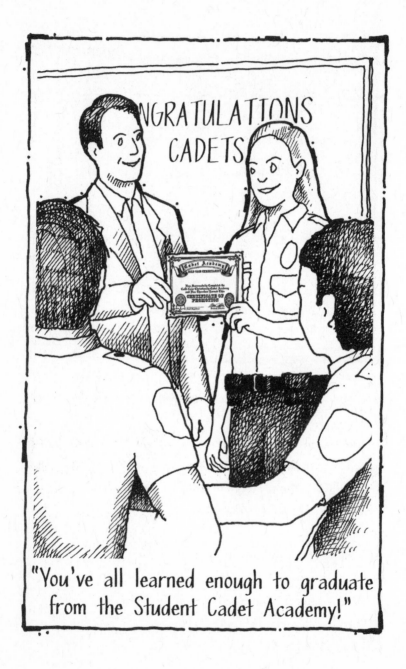

"You've all learned enough to graduate from the Student Cadet Academy!"

POSTSCRIPT

Belief THAT or Belief IN?

All the cadets have graduated, and everyone has left the briefing room now except for you and Jason. He is paging through Detective Jeffries's Bible, waiting for an opportunity to ask a question.

"Based on the evidence, I believe the Bible is telling me the truth about Jesus. Does that mean I'm a Christian?" Jason asks.

"Not necessarily," replies Jeffries as he opens the Bible to the gospel of John chapter 3. "Jesus said there's a difference between belief *that* and belief *in*. Listen to this:

Dig Deep
Visit the
Online Academy

By now you should have completed the activity sheets and fill-ins, so be sure to watch the last video and print out the graduation certificate (or use the one at the end of this book)!

"For God so loved the world, that He gave His only begotten Son, that whoever believes *in* Him shall not perish, but have eternal life" (John 3:16).

Then Jeffries explains, "If you search through the Bible to see what it says about *Jesus*, you'll eventually end up believing *that* Jesus lived, worked miracles, preached sermons, rose from the dead, and is the Son of God. In other words, you'll have 'belief *that*.'" Jeffries continues, "But Jesus said that 'whoever believes *in* Him shall not perish, but have eternal life.' There's a difference." Jeffries points to the open Bible. "To have 'belief *in*,' you need to search through the Bible to see what it says about *you*."

"What do you mean?" inquires Jason.

"Jason," asks Detective Jeffries, "are you a good person?"

Jason thinks about it a minute. "Yes, I try to be."

"Ever make a mistake? Are you perfect?" Jeffries asks.

Jason understands what Jeffries is talking about. "No, I'm not perfect."

Jeffries smiles. "Neither am I. But if there is an all-powerful God who can create everything from nothing, do you think a God like *that* could be *perfect*?"

"Yes, that seems reasonable," says Jason.

Jeffries's expression becomes more serious. "Then there's the problem. If God is perfect, then how can we ever live with Him in eternity when we are *not* perfect? Our *imperfection* would spoil God's *perfection*. The Bible says we are all imperfect, and worse yet, our mistakes, whether large or small, must be punished."

Jason looks a bit worried.

"But here's the good news," adds Jeffries as his serious face turns soft. "The Bible also says God came to us in the form of a man named Jesus. You know, the same one we have been investigating. He lived the perfect life you and I could never live. Then He willingly accepted the punishment *we* deserve. If we accept what Jesus did for us on the cross, God will forgive us since Jesus paid the price for us. When we put our faith and trust *in* Jesus as our Lord and Savior, we finally have 'belief *in*.' See the difference?"

"Yes, I think I get it," answers Jason.

"Great," remarks Jeffries as he gathers up his Bible and the skateboard. "Putting your trust in Jesus is a decision each of us has to make on our own. Give it some thought and then tell God what you've decided. In the meantime, I expect to see both of you here at the station once in a while."

"You will!" you say, as you think deeply about what you've learned from Detective Jeffries.

CSI Assignment

It's time to investigate the gospel. Read Romans 10:9 and think about what God says:

"If you _____ with your mouth Jesus as _____, and _____ in your heart that God raised Him from the dead, you will be _____."

What do you believe about Jesus? Are you ready to accept what Jesus offers?

INSTRUCTIONS FOR USING THE WEBSITE

Be sure to visit www.ColdCaseChristianityforKids.com with your parents to watch the videos for each chapter, download fill-in and activity sheets, and learn how to earn your Academy Promotion Certificate.

A CHALLENGE FROM
J. WARNER WALLACE

I remember when I first investigated the Bible, determined it was true, and trusted Jesus to forgive my sins. It seemed like my life changed immediately. I was *excited* about what I discovered and about what God had done for me. I wanted to tell *everyone* about Jesus.

All my detective partners noticed my enthusiasm right away. At first, they teased me because none of them were Christians. Some thought I was crazy because I had never been interested in God before. I didn't care. I was so happy to finally know the *truth,* and I wanted everyone to hear about the evidence for Jesus.

If you're a Christian, you probably feel the same way. Do you remember how eager you were to tell your friends when you discovered a new hobby? Do you remember how much you wanted them to know about it and join you? That's the feeling I'm talking about. If you're excited to tell your friends about a hobby, you should be even *more* eager to share what you've learned about Jesus! And now you're ready! You've learned enough by reading this book (and completing the worksheets) "to make a defense to everyone who asks you to give an account for the hope that is in you" (1 Peter 3:15).

So I have a simple challenge for you: start making the case! Why wait? There's no better time than *now* to share the good news. Here are some simple ways to get started:

> 1. Show your graduation certificate to your friends and family members. They'll probably ask you how you earned it and you'll be able to tell them about the evidence for Jesus.

> 2. Bring your Academy Notebook to church and show it to friends in your student group or Bible study. Even if they know all about Jesus, they may not know how to be good detectives or how to investigate the evidence for what we believe. Share the case for Jesus with them.

3. Think about your neighborhood friends. Have you ever talked with them about Jesus? You're now ready to start that conversation. It can begin with something as simple as "What do *you* believe about Jesus?"

4. Holiday meals and parties usually involve many family members. Not all of them may believe in Jesus. On the next holiday gathering, show your Certificate and Academy Notebook to your family members and tell them how you earned it and all about the evidence for Jesus.

You're now part of an important team. You're a member of God's family and you're also a graduate of the *Cold-Case Christianity for Kids* Student Cadet Academy. Teams don't just sit on the bench; they *get in the game.* Accept the challenge and start sharing what you've learned with others.

May God be with you as you
share what you've learned,

J. Warner Wallace

As part of your academy training, be sure to complete the Downloadable Fill-In Sheets for each chapter. You can find them at:

www.ColdCaseChristianityforKids.com.

Here are a few of the questions:

Sample Fill-In:
Chapter One - Don't Be A "Know-It-All"

Daniel finds a _____ in the shed.

Daniel thinks it belongs to someone he knows named _____

Why does Daniel think the skateboard belongs to her?

_____

_____

But Detective Jeffries says, "To be a good cold-case detective, you

can't start with your mind _____ "

Jason thinks he has another example of people who seem to be "know-it-alls". What is his example?

_____

_____

Why does Detective Jeffries think Jason may have it "backwards"?

_____

_____

Sample Fill-In:
Chapter Two - Learn How to Infer

Why does Detective Jeffries wear gloves when examining the skateboard?

_____

_____

Detective Jeffries says it's important to remember that many

explanations may be _____, but not every

explanation is _____.

Trying to decide the best explanation from a list of evidences is

called "Abductive _____ ".

List four facts about the Resurrection:

1._____

2._____

3._____

4._____

Chapter Three - Think Circumstantially

Detective Jeffries says there are two ways to find out where the skateboard came from:

(1) Witness evidence is called _____

(2) Everything else is called _____ or
_____ evidence.

Daniel went to Great Skates. What did he learn about the skateboard wheels?

_____

What does this indirect evidence tell us about the age of the board?

_____

Is there any "direct" evidence for God's existence?

Chapter Four - Test Your Witnesses

Four questions we need to ask to find out if a witness can be trusted:

Were they actually _____ ?
Can we _____ what they say in some way?
Have they _____ their story over time?
Do they have some reason to _____ ?

Were the gospels written early? Complete the following timeline:

_____   _____   _____   _____

What two examples does Det. Jeffries give to verify the Gospels?

_____ and _____

Chapter Five - Respect the Chain of Custody

What initials did you find under the sticker on the skateboard?

_____

Did these initials belong to Lincoln?

_____

Who did you, Hannah, and Daniel decide to interview to learn who may have owned the skateboard?

_____

Complete the following "Chain of Custody" for the skateboard:

_____   _____   _____   _____   _____

Chapter Six - Hang On Every Word

Why doesn't Lacey consider herself to be an expert on skateboarding?

_____

_____

But, why did Lacey say she remembered the skateboard?

_____

_____

_____

Detective Jeffries says, "When someone answers a question, listen for _____ they say. But also listen for _____ they say it."

Papias once said Mark wrote the Gospel based on the preaching of _____. In other words, Mark's Gospel is actually _____ eyewitness statement.

Chapter Seven - Separate Artifacts from Evidence

What did Jason find on the skateboard?

_____

Why isn't the paint "evidence" related to the owner of the
skateboard?

_____

_____

According to Detective Jeffries, all crime scenes contain both _____ and

_____ .

We don't have the _____ of the New
Testament Gospels.

Det. Jeffries says, "Scribes made the copies of the original
gospels and sometimes they mistakenly _____ a letter
or a word. Some scribes even added a word or set of words.
They weren't necessarily trying to _____ the message.
Usually they were just trying to make something easier to

_____ ."

Chapter Eight - Resist Conspiracy Theories

What are Jason's remaining doubts about the case
for Jesus?

_____

_____

"But remember what Jeffries said about the fact
that the disciples didn't have a good

_____ ? Why would they all
choose to _____ like they did if they
were only lying?"

Detective Jeffries says,

"_____ occur when groups of people commit a
crime, or tell a lie, and then try to keep the secret
forever. I've investigated many _____ cases,
so I know you need five things to pull one off

_____ ."

(Complete the list on the right:)

1. A small number of _____ .

2. Great _____ .

3. A short _____ .

4. Close _____

5. Low _____ .

Once you've completed *Cold-Case Christianity for Kids* and assembled the Fill-In and Activity Sheets in your Academy Notebook, you're ready to graduate!

There are two ways to get your Certificate of Promotion:

Cut out the 5 x 7 Certificate at the back of this book, add your name, and frame it.

or

Visit the ColdCaseChristianityforKids.com website and print the 8 x 10 Certificate (ask your parents for help if you want to download the customizable version). Add your name, and frame it.

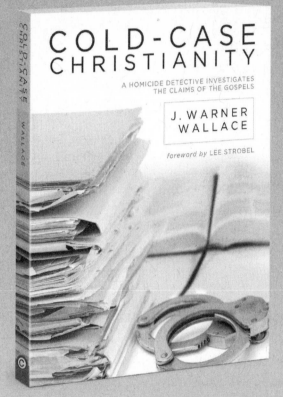

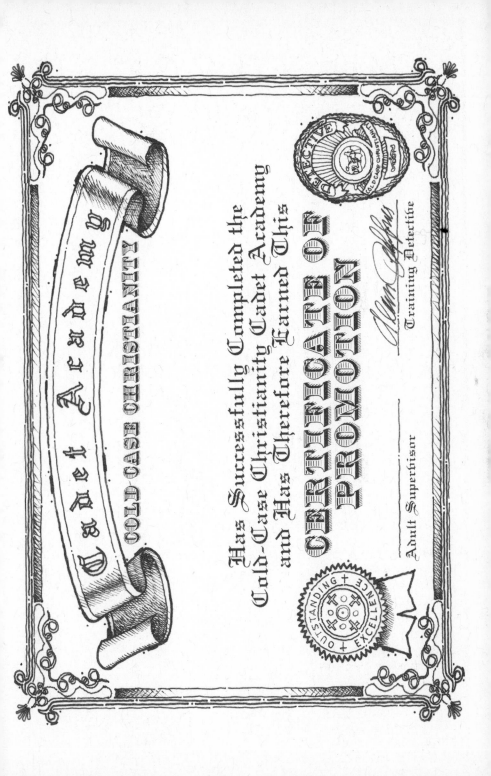

Cadet Academy

COLD-CASE CHRISTIANITY

Has Successfully Completed the
Cold-Case Christianity Cadet Academy
and Has Therefore Earned This

CERTIFICATE OF
PROMOTION

Training Detective

Adult Supervisor